Blessings in Teaching Children

Blessings of Service

TWO COMPILATIONS FROM
THE BAHÁ'Í SACRED WRITINGS

Table of Contents

BLESSINGS IN
TEACHING CHILDREN

BLESSED IS that teacher who remaineth faithful to the Covenant of God, and occupieth himself with the education of children. For him hath the Supreme Pen inscribed that reward which is revealed in the Most Holy Book. Blessed, blessed is he!

Selection I
Bahá'u'lláh
Bahá'í Education
Page 7

BLESSED IS that teacher who shall arise to instruct the children, and to guide the people into the pathways of God, the Bestower, the Well-Beloved.

Selection II
Bahá'u'lláh
Bahá'í Education
Page 7

O YE loving mothers, know ye that in God's sight, the best of all ways to worship Him is to educate the children and train them in all the perfections of humankind; and no nobler deed than this can be imagined.

Selection III
'Abdu'l-Bahá
Selections from the Writings of 'Abdu'l-Bahá
Page 139

NOTES

Selection IV
'Abdu'l-Bahá
Selections from the
Writings of 'Abdu'l-Bahá
Page 138

O HANDMAID of God! ... To the mothers must be given the divine Teachings and effective counsel, and they must be encouraged and made eager to train their children, for the mother is the first educator of the child. It is she who must, at the very beginning, suckle the newborn at the breast of God's Faith and God's Law, that divine love may enter into him even with his mother's milk, and be with him till his final breath.

So long as the mother faileth to train her children, and start them on a proper way of life, the training which they receive later on will not take its full effect. It is incumbent upon the Spiritual Assemblies to provide the mothers with a well-planned programme for the education of children, showing how, from infancy, the child must be watched over and taught. These instructions must be given to every mother to serve her as a guide, so that each will

NOTES

train and nurture her children in accordance
with the Teachings.

WORK YE for the guidance of the women in that
land, teach the young girls and the children,
so that the mothers may educate their little
ones from their earliest days, thoroughly train
them, rear them to have a goodly character and
good morals, guide them to all the virtues of
humankind, prevent the development of any
behaviour that would be worthy of blame, and
foster them in the embrace of Bahá'í education.
Thus shall these tender infants be nurtured at
the breast of the knowledge of God and His
love. Thus shall they grow and flourish, and be
taught righteousness and the dignity of humankind, resolution and the will to strive and to
endure. Thus shall they learn perseverance in
all things, the will to advance, high mindedness
and high resolve, chastity and purity of life.

Selection V
'Abdu'l-Bahá
*Selections from the
Writings of 'Abdu'l-Bahá*
Pages 124–25

NOTES

Thus shall they be enabled to carry to a successful conclusion whatsoever they undertake.

Let the mothers consider that whatever concerneth the education of children is of the first importance. Let them put forth every effort in this regard, for when the bough is green and tender it will grow in whatever way ye train it. Therefore is it incumbent upon the mothers to rear their little ones even as a gardener tendeth his young plants. Let them strive by day and by night to establish within their children faith and certitude, the fear of God, the love of the Beloved of the worlds, and all good qualities and traits. Whensoever a mother seeth that her child hath done well, let her praise and applaud him and cheer his heart; and if the slightest undesirable trait should manifest itself, let her counsel the child and punish him, and use means based on reason, even a slight verbal chastisement should this be necessary. It is not, however, permissible to strike a child, or vilify

NOTES

him, for the child's character will be totally perverted if he be subjected to blows or verbal abuse.

O HANDMAIDS of the Merciful! Render ye thanks unto the Ancient Beauty that ye have been raised up and gathered together in this mightiest of centuries, this most illumined of ages. As befitting thanks for such a bounty, stand ye staunch and strong in the Covenant and, following the precepts of God and the holy Law, suckle your children from their infancy with the milk of a universal education, and rear them so that from their earliest days, within their inmost heart, their very nature, a way of life will be firmly established that will conform to the divine Teachings in all things.

For mothers are the first educators, the first mentors; and truly it is the mothers who determine the happiness, the future greatness, the courteous ways and learning and judge-

Selection VI
'Abdu'l-Bahá
Selections from the Writings of 'Abdu'l-Bahá
Pages 125–26

NOTES

ment, the understanding and the faith of their little ones.

Selection VII
‘Abdu’l-Bahá
Selections from the Writings of ‘Abdu’l-Bahá
Pages 126–27

WERE THERE no educator, all souls would remain savage, and were it not for the teacher, the children would be ignorant creatures.

It is for this reason that, in this new cycle, education and training are recorded in the Book of God as obligatory and not voluntary. That is, it is enjoined upon the father and mother, as a duty, to strive with all effort to train the daughter and the son, to nurse them from the breast of knowledge and to rear them in the bosom of sciences and arts. Should they neglect this matter, they shall be held responsible and worthy of reproach in the presence of the stern Lord.

NOTES

O YE who have peace of soul! Among the divine Texts as set forth in the Most Holy Book and also in other Tablets is this: it is incumbent upon the father and mother to train their children both in good conduct and the study of books; study, that is, to the degree required, so that no child, whether girl or boy, will remain illiterate. Should the father fail in his duty he must be compelled to discharge his responsibility, and should he be unable to comply, let the House of Justice take over the education of the children; in no case is a child to be left without an education. This is one of the stringent and inescapable commandments to neglect which would draw down the wrathful indignation of Almighty God.

Selection VIII
'Abdu'l-Bahá
Selections from the Writings of 'Abdu'l-Bahá
Pages 127–28

NOTES

Selection IX
'Abdu'l-Bahá
Bahá'í Education
Page 25

O STEADFAST in the Covenant! . Praise thou God that thou hast succeeded in becoming a teacher of young Bahá'ís, young trees of the Abhá Paradise, and at the same time art able to benefit the other children as well.

According to the explicit divine Text, teaching the children is indispensable and obligatory. It followeth that teachers are servants of the Lord God, since they have arisen to perform this task, which is the same as worship. You must therefore offer praise with every breath, for you are educating your spiritual children.

The spiritual father is greater than the physical one, for the latter bestoweth but this world's life, whereas the former endoweth his child with life everlasting. This is why, in the Law of God, teachers are listed among the heirs.

NOTES

Now you in reality have acquired all these spiritual children free and gratis, and that is better than having physical children; for such children are not grateful to their fathers, since they feel that the father serveth them because he must—and therefore no matter what he doeth for them, they pay it no mind. Spiritual children, however, are always appreciative of their father's loving kindness. This verily is out of the grace of thy Lord, the Beneficent.

O SERVANT of the Blessed Beauty!

Blessed art thou, since thou art engaged in rendering a service which will make thy face to shine in the Abhá Kingdom, and that is the education and training of children. If one should, in the right way, teach and train the children, he will be performing a service than which none is greater at the Sacred Threshold.

Selection X
'Abdu'l-Bahá
Bahá'í Education
Page 24

NOTES

According to what we have heard, you are succeeding in this. You must, however, struggle unceasingly to perfect yourself and win ever higher achievements.

At all times, I implore Almighty God to make you the means of illuminating the minds of those children, of bringing their hearts to life and sanctifying their souls.

Selection XI
'Abdu'l-Bahá
Bahá'í Education
Pages 25–6

O THOU who art steadfast in the Covenant! Thou hast exerted strenuous efforts for the education of children and I have been, and am, infinitely pleased with thee. Praise God, thou hast been enabled to serve in this field, and it is certain that the confirmations of the Abhá Kingdom will encompass thee, and thou shalt achieve prosperity and success.

Today the training and education of the believers' children is the pre-eminent goal of the chosen. It is the same as servitude to the Sacred Threshold and waiting upon the Blessed

NOTES

Beauty. Joyously, therefore, canst thou pride thyself on this.

ONE OF the most important of undertakings is the education of children, for success and prosperity depend upon service to and worship of God, the Holy, the All-Glorified.

Among the greatest of all great services is the education of children. Praised be God, ye are now exerting strenuous efforts toward this end. The more ye persevere in this most important task, the more will ye witness the confirmations of God, to such a degree that ye yourselves will be astonished.

This verily is a matter beyond all doubt, a pledge that shall certainly be redeemed.

Selection XII
'Abdu'l-Bahá
Bahá'í Education
Page 27

NOTES

Selection XIII
'Abdu'l-Bahá
Bahá'í Education
Page 26

O THOU teacher of the children of the kingdom!

Thou hast arisen to perform a service which would justly entitle thee to vaunt thyself over all the teachers on earth. For the teachers of this world make use of human education to develop the powers, whether spiritual or material, of humankind, whilst thou art training these young plants in the gardens of God according to the education of Heaven, and art giving them the lessons of the Kingdom.

The result of this kind of teaching will be that it will attract the blessings of God, and make manifest the perfections of man.

Hold thou fast to this kind of teaching, for the fruits of it will be very great. The children must, from their infancy, be raised to be spiritual and godly Bahá'ís. If such be their training, they will remain safe from every test.

NOTES

AMONG THE greatest of all services that can possibly be rendered by man to Almighty God is the education and training of children, young plants of the Abhá Paradise, so that these children, fostered by grace in the way of salvation, growing like pearls of divine bounty in the shell of education, will one day bejewel the crown of abiding glory.

It is, however, very difficult to undertake this service, even harder to succeed in it. I hope that thou wilt acquit thyself well in this most important of tasks, and successfully carry the day, and become an ensign of God's abounding grace; that these children, reared one and all in the holy Teachings, will develop natures like unto the sweet airs that blow across the gardens of the All-Glorious, and will waft their fragrance around the world.

Selection XIV
'Abdu'l-Bahá
Selections from the
Writings of 'Abdu'l-Bahá
Pages 133–34

NOTES

Selection XV
'Abdu'l-Bahá
Bahá'í Education
Pages 24–5

O THOU spiritual teacher! Be thou a teacher of love, in a school of unity. Train thou the children of the friends of the Merciful in the rules and ways of His loving-kindness. Tend the young trees of the Abhá Paradise with the welling waters of His grace and peace and joy. Make them to flourish under the downpour of His bounty. Strive with all thy powers that the children may stand out and grow fresh, delicate, and sweet, like the ideal trees in the gardens of Heaven.

All these gifts and bounties depend upon love for the Beauty of the All-Glorious, and on the blessings in the teachings of the Most High, and the spiritual instructions of the Supreme Concourse, and on ecstasy and ardour and diligent pursuit of whatsoever will redound to the eternal honour of the community of man.

NOTES

O YE two well-loved handmaids of God! Whatever a man's tongue speaketh, that let him prove by his deeds. If he claimeth to be a believer, then let him act in accordance with the precepts of the Abhá Kingdom.

Praised be God, ye two have demonstrated the truth of your words by your deeds, and have won the confirmations of the Lord God. Every day at first light, ye gather the Bahá'í children together and teach them the communes and prayers. This is a most praiseworthy act, and bringeth joy to the children's hearts: that they should, at every morn, turn their faces toward the Kingdom and make mention of the Lord and praise His Name, and in the sweetest of voices, chant and recite.

These children are even as young plants, and teaching them the prayers is as letting the rain pour down upon them, that they may wax tender and fresh, and the soft breezes of the

Selection XVI
'Abdu'l-Bahá
Selections from the Writings of 'Abdu'l-Bahá
Page 139

NOTES

love of God may blow over them, making them to tremble with joy.

Blessedness awaiteth you, and a fair haven.

Selection XVII
'Abdu'l-Bahá
Selections from the
Writings of 'Abdu'l-Bahá
Pages 129–31

THE EDUCATION and training of children is among the most meritorious acts of humankind and draweth down the grace and favour of the All-Merciful, for education is the indispensable foundation of all human excellence and alloweth man to work his way to the heights of abiding glory. If a child be trained from his infancy, he will, through the loving care of the Holy Gardener, drink in the crystal waters of the spirit and of knowledge, like a young tree amid the rolling brooks. And certainly he will gather to himself the bright rays of the Sun of Truth, and through its light and heat will grow ever fresh and fair in the garden of life.

NOTES

Therefore must the mentor be a doctor as well: that is, he must, in instructing the child, remedy its faults; must give him learning, and at the same time rear him to have a spiritual nature. Let the teacher be a doctor to the character of the child, thus will he heal the spiritual ailments of the children of men.

If, in this momentous task, a mighty effort be exerted, the world of humanity will shine out with other adornings, and shed the fairest light. Then will this darksome place grow luminous, and this abode of earth turn into Heaven. The very demons will change to angels then, and wolves to shepherds of the flock, and the wild-dog pack to gazelles that pasture on the plains of oneness, and ravening beasts to peaceful herds; and birds of prey, with talons sharp as knives, to songsters warbling their sweet native notes.

NOTES

Every child is potentially the light of the world—and at the same time its darkness; wherefore must the question of education be accounted as of primary importance. From his infancy, the child must be nursed at the breast of God's love, and nurtured in the embrace of His knowledge, that he may radiate light, grow in spirituality, be filled with wisdom and learning, and take on the characteristics of the angelic host.

Since ye have been assigned to this holy task, ye must therefore exert every effort to make that school famed in all respects throughout the world; to make it the cause of exalting the Word of the Lord.

Selection XVIII
'Abdu'l-Bahá
Bahá'í Education
Page 25

ESTABLISH SCHOOLS that are well organized, and promote the fundamentals of instruction in the various branches of knowledge through teachers who are pure and sanctified, distinguished for their high standards of conduct and

NOTES

general excellence, and strong in faith; educators with a thorough knowledge of sciences and arts.

THERE ARE certain pillars which have been established as the unshakeable supports of the Faith of God. The mightiest of these is learning and the use of the mind, the expansion of consciousness, and insight into the realities of the universe and the hidden mysteries of Almighty God.

Selection XIX
'Abdu'l-Bahá
Selections from the Writings of 'Abdu'l-Bahá
Pages126

To promote knowledge is thus an inescapable duty imposed on every one of the friends of God. It is incumbent upon that Spiritual Assembly, that assemblage of God, to exert every effort to educate the children, so that from infancy they will be trained in Bahá'í conduct and the ways of God, and will, even as young plants, thrive and flourish in the soft-flowing waters that are the counsels and admonitions of the Blessed Beauty.

NOTES

BLESSINGS OF SERVICE

THE FIRST duty prescribed by God for His servants is the recognition of Him Who is the Dayspring of His Revelation and the Fountain of His laws, Who representeth the Godhead in both the Kingdom of His Cause and the world of creation. Whoso achieveth this duty hath attained unto all good; and whoso is deprived thereof hath gone astray, though he be the author of every righteous deed. It behoveth everyone who reacheth this most sublime station, this summit of transcendent glory, to observe every ordinance of Him Who is the Desire of the world. These twin duties are inseparable. Neither is acceptable without the other. Thus hath it been decreed by Him Who is the Source of Divine inspiration.

Selection I
Bahá'u'lláh
Kitáb-i-Aqdas
Page 19

NOTES

Selection II
Bahá'u'lláh
Quoted in a letter of the
Universal House of Justice
to the Bahá'ís of the World
Ridván 1982

BLESSED IS he who in the prime of his youth and the heyday of his life will arise to serve the Cause of the Lord of the beginning and of the end …. Blessed are the steadfast and well is it with those who are firm.

Selection III
Bahá'u'lláh
Gleanings from the Writ-
ings of Bahá'u'lláh
Pages 334–35

HOW GREAT the blessedness that awaiteth him that hath attained the honor of serving the Almighty! By My life! No act, however great, can compare with it, except such deeds as have been ordained by God, the All-Powerful, the Most Mighty. Such a service is, indeed, the prince of all goodly deeds, and the ornament of every goodly act. Thus hath it been ordained by Him Who is the Sovereign Revealer, the Ancient of Days …. Happy is the man that hath heard Our voice, and answered Our call. He, in truth, is of them that shall be brought nigh unto Us.

NOTES

THIS IS the day to make mention of God, to celebrate His praise, and to serve Him; deprive not yourselves thereof. Ye are the letters of the words, and the words of the Book. Ye are the saplings which the hand of Loving-kindness hath planted in the soil of mercy, and which the showers of bounty have made to flourish. He hath protected you from the mighty winds of misbelief, and the tempestuous gales of impiety, and nurtured you with the hands of His loving providence. Now is the time for you to put forth your leaves, and yield your fruit.

Selection IV
Bahá'u'lláh
Epistle to the Son of the Wolf
Pages 25–6

O YE beloved of God! Repose not yourselves on your couches, nay bestir yourselves as soon as ye recognize your Lord, the Creator, and hear of the things which have befallen Him, and hasten to His assistance. Unloose your tongues, and proclaim unceasingly His Cause. This shall be better for you than all the treasures of the

Selection V
Bahá'u'lláh
Gleanings from the Writings of Bahá'u'lláh
Page 330

NOTES

past and of the future, if ye be of them that comprehend this truth.

Selection VI
Bahá'u'lláh
Gleanings from the Writings of Bahá'u'lláh
Pages 196–97

O FRIENDS! Be not careless of the virtues with which ye have been endowed, neither be neglectful of your high destiny. Suffer not your labors to be wasted through the vain imaginations which certain hearts have devised. Ye are the stars of the heaven of understanding, the breeze that stirreth at the break of day, the soft-flowing waters upon which must depend the very life of all men, the letters inscribed upon His sacred scroll. With the utmost unity, and in a spirit of perfect fellowship, exert yourselves, that ye may be enabled to achieve that which beseemeth this Day of God. Verily I say, strife and dissension, and whatsoever the mind of man abhorreth are entirely unworthy of his station. Center your energies in the propagation of the Faith of God. Whoso is worthy of so high a calling, let him arise and promote it.

NOTES

WHOSO IS unable, it is his duty to appoint him who will, in his stead, proclaim this Revelation, whose power hath caused the foundations of the mightiest structures to quake, every mountain to be crushed into dust, and every soul to be dumbfounded. Should the greatness of this Day be revealed in its fullness, every man would forsake a myriad lives in his longing to partake, though it be for one moment, of its great glory - how much more this world and its corruptible treasures!

IT IS incumbent upon every man of insight and understanding to strive to translate that which hath been written into reality and action .... That one indeed is a man who, today, dedicateth himself to the service of the entire human race. The Great Being saith: Blessed and happy is he that ariseth to promote the best interests of the peoples and kindreds of the earth.

Selection VII
Bahá'u'lláh
Gleanings from the Writings of Bahá'u'lláh
Page 250

NOTES

Selection VIII
Bahá'u'lláh
Gleanings from the Writings of Bahá'u'lláh
Page 110

BLESSED ARE they that remember the one true God, that magnify His Name, and seek diligently to serve His Cause. It is to these men that the sacred Books of old have referred. On them hath the Commander of the Faithful lavished his praise, saying: "The blessedness awaiting them excelleth the blessedness we now enjoy." He, verily, hath spoken the truth, and to this We now testify. The glory of their station, however, is as yet undisclosed. The Hand of Divine power will, assuredly, lift up the veil, and expose to the sight of men that which shall cheer and lighten the eye of the world.

Render thanks unto God ... inasmuch as ye have attained so wondrous a favor, and been adorned with the ornament of His praise. Appreciate the value of these days, and cleave to whatsoever beseemeth this Revelation.

NOTES

HAPPY IS the man who will arise to serve My Cause, and glorify My beauteous Name. Take hold of My Book with the power of My might, and cleave tenaciously to whatsoever commandment thy Lord, the Ordainer, the All-Wise, hath prescribed therein.

Selection IX
Bahá'u'lláh
Gleanings from the Writings of Bahá'u'lláh
Page 69

WHEN THE victory arriveth, every man shall profess himself as believer and shall hasten to the shelter of God's Faith. Happy are they who in the days of world-encompassing trials have stood fast in the Cause and refused to swerve from its truth.

Selection X
Bahá'u'lláh
Gleanings from the Writings of Bahá'u'lláh
Page 319

BLESSED ARE they that have soared on the wings of detachment and attained the station which, as ordained by God, overshadoweth the entire creation, whom neither the vain imaginations of the learned, nor the multitude of the hosts of the earth have succeeded in deflecting from His Cause. Who is there among you, O

Selection XI
Bahá'u'lláh
Gleanings from the Writings of Bahá'u'lláh
Pages 34–5

NOTES

people, who will renounce the world, and draw nigh unto God, the Lord of all names? Where is he to be found who, through the power of My name that transcendeth all created things, will cast away the things that men possess, and cling, with all his might, to the things which God, the Knower of the unseen and of the seen, hath bidden him observe? Thus hath His bounty been sent down unto men, His testimony fulfilled, and His proof shone forth above the Horizon of mercy. Rich is the prize that shall be won by him who hath believed and exclaimed: "Lauded art Thou, O Beloved of all worlds! Magnified be Thy name, O Thou the Desire of every understanding heart!"

Selection XII
Bahá'u'lláh
Proclamation of Bahá'u'lláh
Page 116

BLESSED AND happy is he that ariseth to promote the best interests of the peoples and kindreds of the earth.

NOTES

O MY handmaiden, O My leaf! Render thou thanks unto the Best-Beloved of the world for having attained this boundless grace at a time when the world's learned and most distinguished men have remained deprived thereof. We have designated thee 'a leaf' that thou mayest, like unto leaves, be stirred by the gentle wind of the Will of God ... even as the leaves of the trees are stirred by onrushing winds. Yield thou thanks unto thy Lord by virtue of this brilliant utterance. Wert thou to perceive the sweetness of the title 'O My handmaiden' thou wouldst find thyself detached from all mankind, devoutly engaged day and night in communion with Him Who is the sole Desire of the world.

In words of incomparable beauty We have made fitting mention of such leaves and handmaidens as have quaffed from the living waters of heavenly grace and have kept their eyes directed towards God. Happy and blessed

Selection XIII
Bahá'u'lláh
Tablets of Bahá'u'lláh
Pages 254–55

NOTES

are they indeed. Ere long shall God reveal their station whose loftiness no word can befittingly express nor any description adequately describe.

We admonish thee to do that which will serve to promote the interests of the Cause of God amongst men and women. He doth hear the call of the friends and beholdeth their actions.

Selection XIV
Bahá'u'lláh
Tablets of Bahá'u'lláh
Pages 257–58

HAPPY IS the faithful one who is attired with the vesture of high endeavour and hath arisen to serve this Cause. Such a soul hath truly attained the desired Goal and hath apprehended the Object for which it hath been created. But a myriad times alas for the wayward who are like unto dried-up leaves fallen upon the dust. Ere long mortal blasts shall carry them away to the place ordained for them. Ignorant did they arrive, ignorant did they linger and ignorant did they retire to their abodes .... It behoveth the people of Bahá to invoke and entreat the

NOTES

Lord of Names that perchance the people of the world may not be deprived of the effusions of grace in His days.

GREAT IS thy blessedness inasmuch as thou hast been faithful to the Covenant of God and His Testament .... Dedicate thyself to the service of the Cause of thy Lord, cherish His remembrance in thy heart and celebrate His praise in such wise that every wayward and heedless soul may thereby be roused from slumber."

Selection XV
Bahá'u'lláh
Tablets of Bahá'u'lláh
Page 262

NOTES

www.ingramcontent.com/pod-product-compliance
Lightning Source LLC
Chambersburg PA
CBHW060546030426
42337CB00021B/4451